Anatomy Under the Sea: The Adventures of Luna the Loggerhead

Written by: Emiliana Fuger

Illustrations by: Jess Burbank

Published by Orange Hat Publishing 2026
SC ISBN: 978164538630
HC ISBN: 9781645386315
LCCN: 2025913760

Copyright © 2026 by Emiliana Fuger
All Rights Reserved
Anatomy Under the Sea
Written by Emiliana Fuger
Illustrated by Jess Burbank
This publication and all contents within may not be reproduced or transmitted in any part or in its entirety without the written permission of the author.

orangehatpublishing.com

Dedicated to
all the kids that love the ocean!

Once upon a time,
in the ocean so wide,
lived a little sea turtle
full of joy and pride.

Her name was Luna the Loggerhead, and she was a peach. Ready to lay her eggs in the soft, sandy Juno Beach.

She began her long journey through the warm Atlantic Ocean. Visiting friends along the way, she was filled with such emotion.

Swimming along, who does she see?
Henry the Hammerhead Shark, cruising wild and free.
"Hello, Henry, my ocean friend, so dear!
What anatomy will we learn about here?"

"Your sixth sense helps you find the beach,
even when it seems out of reach.
I have a sixth sense too, that helps me take heed
of animals nearby on which to feed."

Swimming along,
who does she see?
Marah the Manta Ray,
gliding wild and free.
"Hello, Marah,
my ocean friend, so dear!
What anatomy will we
learn about here?"

"We both have babies
that fill us with glee.
Mine are born alive and in the sea.
Yours are born from shells in the sand,
but both our Cloacas help things
go as planned."

Swimming along, who does she see?
Jemma the Jellyfish, drifting wild and free.
"Hello, Jemma, my ocean friend, so dear!
What anatomy will we learn about here?"

"I'm a simple creature without blood, a brain, or a heart.
My nervous system is what gives me my start.
We both like to fill our bellies, but you eat on the reef.
So how about you find a crab for some relief?"

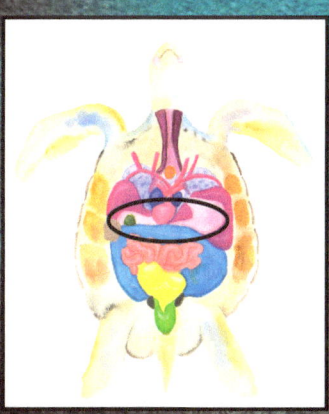

Swimming along, who does she see?
Adrian the Seahorse, floating wild and free.
"Hello, Adrian, my ocean friend, so dear!
What anatomy will we learn about here?"

"As a mama sea turtle,
you lay eggs for your babies to grow.
They emerge from the sand, ready to go.
As a daddy seahorse,
my job is different, you see.
The babies grow in my pouch
until they are ready to swim free."

Swimming along, who does she see?
Sol the Sea Star, resting wild and free.
"Hello, Sol, my ocean friend, so dear!
What anatomy will we learn about here?"

"I lost an arm, but that is ok.
It'll grow back in a couple of days.
Your flippers can't grow back; that much is clear,
But with the help of some human friends,
you'll swim again - have no fear!"

Swimming along, who does she see?
Oliver the Octopus, roaming wild and free.
"Hello, Oliver, my ocean friend, so dear!
What anatomy will we learn about here?"

"I've got three hearts
and nine brains, it's true.
With blue blood flowing,
I'm not like you.
But with one heart and one brain,
you're just as great.
We're both unique,
and that's something to celebrate!"

Swimming along, who does she see?
Eva the Manatee, playing wild and free.
"Hello, Eva, my ocean friend, so dear!
What anatomy will we learn about here?"

Swimming along, who does she see?
Charlie the Horseshoe Crab, crawling wild and free.
"Hello, Charlie, my ocean friend, so dear!
What anatomy will we learn about here?"

"We both have shells that protect us and are strong.
Yours stays with you your whole life long.
My shell is great, but as I grow, it sheds,
giving me a bigger space to stretch my legs."

As Luna reached the beach,
she was happy under the sun.
Her journey was at an end,
but the job was not done.

She waited until night to swim up onto the shore. Carefully picking the right spot, where she had been born before.

With her eggs buried safely in the sand,
Luna returned to the ocean so grand.

Internal Anatomy of a Sea Turtle

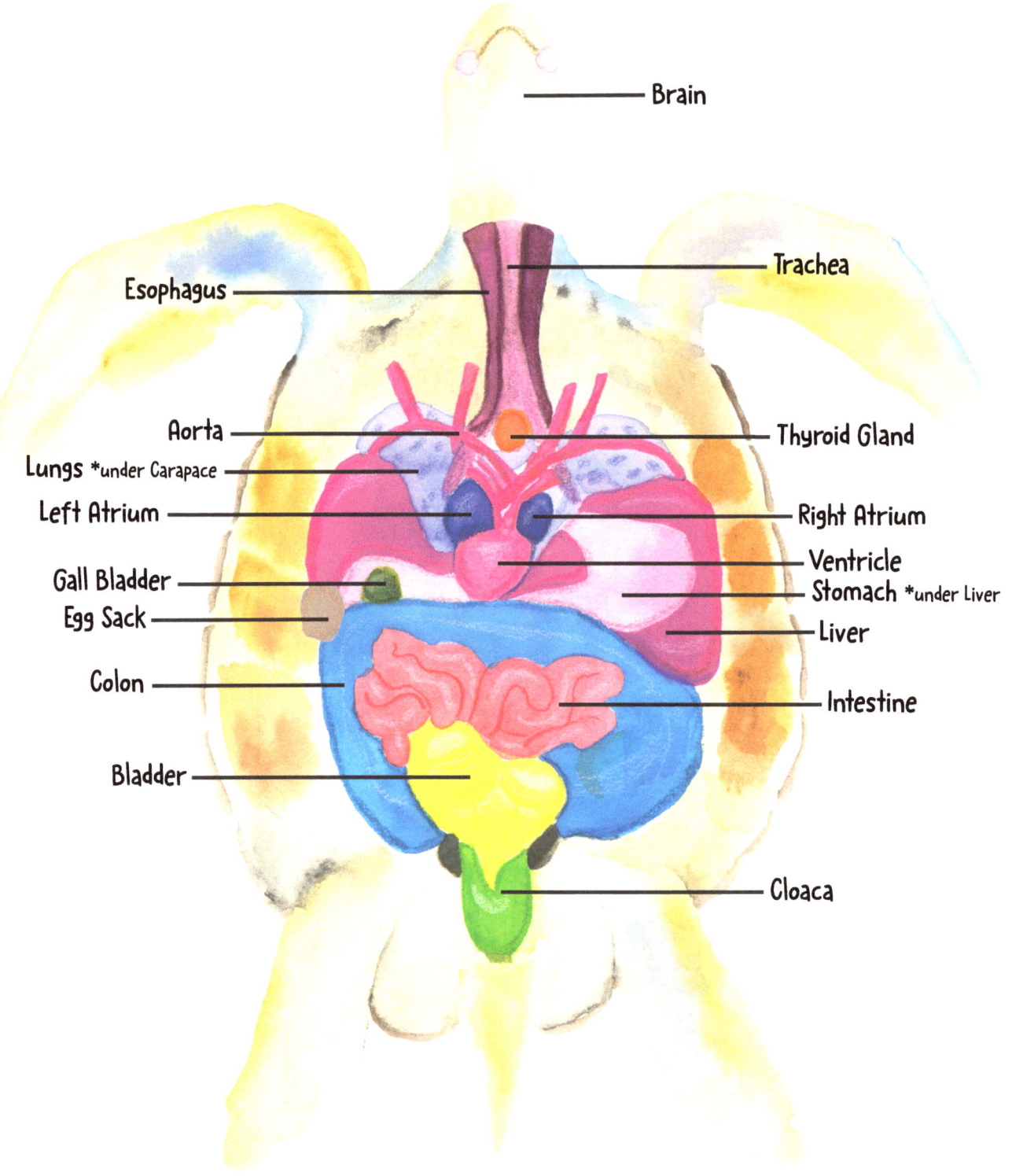

Reference: Boyer, T.H. and Innis, C.J. "Chelonian Taxonomy, Anatomy, and Physiology" in Mader's Reptile and Amphibian Medicine and Surgery, edited by S. Divers and S. Stahl. Elsevier, 2018.

Marine Animal Size Chart

 Giant Manta Ray: 22-29ft

Great Hammerhead Shark: 12-20ft

 West Indian Manatee: 9-13ft

Loggerhead Sea Turtle: 2-4ft

 Atlantic Horseshoe Crab: 14-24in

Red Cushion Sea Star: 10-20in

 Atlantic Longarm Octopus: body 2-3.5in, arms 8-9in

Moon Jelly: 2-16in

Lined Seahorse: 5-6in

Definitions

ANATOMY
The science that studies the structure of the body.

BUOYANCY
The ability of a body to float or rise when submerged in water.

CLOACA
The common cavity into which the intestinal, urinary, and reproductive tracts open in reptiles and other animals; is the opening through which sea turtle eggs are laid.

FLIPPERS
The large, flat front feet that help sea turtles swim and move on the sand.

LUNA
The Spanish word for moon.

NERVOUS SYSTEM
The primary means of processing sensory information and coordinating movement.

SOL
The Spanish word for sun.

Special Thanks!

First and most importantly, I would like to thank my parents, my Abi, and my whole family for encouraging me to dream big and keep trying with this project. To my 3rd grade teacher Ms Anelize Core and my assistant principal Ms Monica Anthony for always being my cheerleaders to keep going.

Thank you to Gabrielle Raymond McGee, Dr. Sylvia Earle, and everyone at Wavemakers for helping bring Luna to life. Also, thank you to the volunteers of Sea Turtle Adventures for having us on their nest excavations since 2022.

Lastly, thank you to the scientists and docents who took the time to talk with me and answer all my questions, including:
- Dr. Chelsea Bennice of FAU Marine Lab and OctoNation
- Doris of John D McArther State Park
- Hanna Medd of American Shark Conservancy
- Isabelle of Manatee Lagoon
- Jordan Ferre of Loggerhead MarineLife Center
- Jillian Morris of Sharks for Kids
- Olivia of Florida Manta Project

Photo Courtesy of Cara Moriarty Photography

Meet the Author

Emiliana Fuger is a 9-year-old from Wellington, FL, who loves her family and loyal pup Jemma, celebrating her Hispanic heritage, and spending time by the ocean. She finds joy in snorkeling at Phil Foster Park, where she discovers vibrant marine life beneath the waves. When she's on land, she keeps busy with school and many extracurricular activities. As a 2025 Wavemakers Competition Winner, 2025 Go Blue Awards Finalist, and 2024 Wavemakers Competition Finalist, she's so excited to share Luna and her friends with other curious kids! Read more about her story at www.LunatheLoggerhead.com

Meet the Illustrator

Jess Burbank is a picture book author and illustrator, working primarily with traditional media daily from her art studio in Bellevue, WA. She grew up in Ft. Myers, FL, and misses the beach, but now enjoys nature walks to admire the beauty of the Pacific Northwest with her husband, two kids, and corgi. Find more of her work at www.jessburbank.com

www.ingramcontent.com/pod-product-compliance
Lightning Source LLC
LaVergne TN
LVHW071033070426
835507LV00003B/136